A Garland Series

The English Stage
Attack and Defense 1577 - 1730

A collection of 90 important works
reprinted in photo-facsimile in 50 volumes

edited by
Arthur Freeman
Boston University

A Short Vindication
of the *Relapse*
and the *Provok'd Wife*

by

John Vanbrugh

with a preface
for the Garland Edition by

Arthur Freeman

Garland Publishing, Inc., New York & London

1972

Library of Congress Cataloging in Publication Data

Vanbrugh, Sir John, 1664-1726.
  A short vindication of The relapse and The provok'd
wife.

  (The English stage: attack and defense, 1577-1730)
  Reprint of the 1698 ed.
  "Wing V59."
  1. Collier, Jeremy, 1650-1726. A short view of the
immorality and profaneness of the English stage.
2. Theater--Moral and religious aspects. 3. Theater--
England. I. Title. II. Series.
PN2047.C62V3 1972   792'.013   75-170442
ISBN 0-8240-0612-7

Preface

Perhaps singly the most important, if oddly one of the least telling replies to Collier was by the architect of weighty Blenheim and author of the effervescent Relapse, *Sir John Vanbrugh, whose arguments in favor of his comic intent are oddly sententious, and lend far too much dignity to his assailant's blunt approach to succeed in dismissing him within five sheets. Joseph Wood Krutch (*Conscience and Comedy *[1949], pp. 122 ff.) deals respectfully with Vanbrugh's essentially moral and aesthetic counters (of which one may particularize his points that Collier was nearly blind to satire, and inevitably attributes convenient opinions voiced by any dramatic character in any context to the author himself — shades of succeeding Shakespearean criticism!), but the pamphlet leaves us uneasily suspicious that the wittier and wiser Vanbrugh had pitched his reply unprofitably higher than the plain style of his forceful opponent. Haste may account for some stuntedness:* A Vindication *was first advertised*

PREFACE

9-11 June 1698, less than two months after the appearance of A Short View; *it has been reasonably argued as well that Vanbrugh himself was not wholly sensitive to the moral tenor of his own writings as they struck contemporaries and strike us. The latter is by no means impossible, and may account for the almost tortured sincerity of the present reply, where a month later William Congreve offered — perhaps weakly as well — ridicule, rhetoric, and a lofty disdain for the dullness of Jeremy Collier.*

Our reprint of A Vindication *is prepared from a copy of the original edition in the possession of the Publishers, collating $A\text{-}E^8 F^2$ (lacking the half-title, A1, supplied from a copy at Yale [Haf 21 707f]). Lowe-Arnott-Robinson 319; Hooker 8; Wing V59; Ashley VII, 178.*

July, 1972   A. F.

6

A

Short Vindication

OF THE

Relapse, and the *Provok'd Wife.*

A

Short Vindication

OF THE

RELAPSE

AND THE

Provok'd Wife,

FROM

Immorality and Prophaneſs

By the AUTHOR.

LONDON:
Printed for H. Walwyn, at the *Three Legs* in the *Poultrey*, againſt the *Stocks-Market*. MDCXCVIII.

A Short Vindication of the Relapse and the Provok'd Wife, from Immorality and Prophaneness.

WHEN firſt I ſaw Mr. *Collier*'s Performance upon the Irregularities of the Stage (in which amongſt the reſt of the Gentlemen, he's pleas'd to afford me ſome particular Favours), I was far from deſigning to trouble either my ſelf or the Town with a Vindication; I thought his Charges againſt me for Immorality and Prophaneneſs were grounded upon ſo much Miſtake, that every one (who had had the curioſity to ſee the Plays, or on

A 3   this

this Occasion should take the trouble to read 'em) would easily discover the Root of the Invective, and that 'twas the Quarrel of his Gown, and not of his God, that made him take Arms against me.

I found the Opinion of my Friends and Acquaintance the same, (at least they told me so) and the Righteous as well as the Unrighteous persuaded me, The Attack was so weak, the Town wou'd defend it self; That the General's Head was too hot for his Conduct to be wise; his Shot too much at Random ever to make a Breach; and that the Siege wou'd be raised, without my taking the Field.

I easily believ'd, what my Laziness made me wish; but I have since found, That by the Industry of some People, whose Temporal Interest engages 'em in the Squabble;

ble; and the Natural Propensity of others, to be fond of any thing that's Abusive; this Lampoon has got Credit enough in some Places to brand the Persons it mentions with almost as bad a Character, as the Author of it has fixt upon himself, by his Life and Conversation in the World.

I think 'tis therefore now a thing no farther to be laught at. Should I wholly sit still, those People who are so much mistaken to think I have been busy to encourage Immorality, may double their Mistake, and fancy I profess it: I will therefore endeavour, in a very few Pages to convince the World, I have brought nothing upon the Stage, that proves me more an Atheist than a Bigot.

I may be blind in what relates to my self; 'tis more than possible, for most People are so: But

if

if I judge right, what I have done is in general a Discouragement to Vice and Folly; I am sure I intended it, and I hope I have performed it. Perhaps I have not gone the common Road, nor observed the strictest Prescriptions: But I believe those who know this Town, will agree, That the Rules of a College of Divines will in an Infinity of Cases, fall as short of the Disorders of the Mind, as those of the Physicians do in the Diseases of the Body; and I think a man may vary from 'em both, without being a Quack in either.

The real Query is, Whether the Way I have varied, be likely to have a good Effect, or a bad one? That's the true State of the Case; which if I am cast in, I don't question however to gain at least thus much of my Cause, That it shall be allow'd I aim'd at

the

the Mark, whether I hit it or not.
This, if it won't vindicate my
Senfe, will juftify my Morals;
and fhew the World, That this
Honeft Gentleman, in ftretching
his Malice, and curtailing his Charity, has play'd a Part which
wou'd have much better become
a Licentious Poet, than a Reverend Divine.

Tho' I refolve to ufe very few
Words, I would willingly obferve
fome Method, were it poffible;
that the World, who is the Judge,
might fum up the Evidence the
eafier, and bring the Right and
Wrong into the fhorter (and by
confequence the clearer) View:
But his Play is fo wild, I muft be
content to take the Ball as it comes,
and return it if I can; which whether I always do or not, however,
I believe will prove no great matter, fince I hope 'twill appear,
where

where he gives me the Reft; he makes but a wide Chace: His moft threatning Strokes end in nothing at all; when he Cuts, he's under Line; when he Forces, he's up in the Nets. But to leave Tennis, and come to the Matter.

The Firft Chapter in his Book is upon the Immodefty of the Stage; where he tells you how valuable a Qualification Modefty is in a Woman: For my part I am wholly of his mind; I think 'tis almoft as valuable in a Woman as in a Clergyman; and had I the ruling of the Roaft, the one fhou'd neither have a Husband, nor the t'other a Benefice without it. If this Declaration won't ferve to fhew I'm a Friend to't, let us fee what Proof this Gentleman can give of the contrary.

I don't

I don't find him over-stock'd with Quotations in this Chapter: He's forc'd, rather than say nothing, to fall upon poor Miss *Hoy-* P. 10. *den.* He does not come to Particulars, but only mentions her with others, for an immodest Character. What kind of Immodesty he means, I can't tell: But I suppose he means Lewdness, because he generally means wrong. For my part, I know of no Bawdy she talks: If the Strength of his Imagination gives any of her Discourse that Turn, I suppose it may be owing to the Number of Bawdy Plays he has read, which have debauch'd his Taste, and made every thing seem Salt, that comes in his way.

He has but one Quotation more in this long Chapter, that I am P. 35. concern'd in: And there he points at the *Provok'd Wife*, as if there

were

were something in the 41ſt Page
of that Play, to diſcountenance
Modeſty in Women. But ſince
he did not think fit to acquaint the
Reader what it was, I will.

Lady *Brute* and *Bellinda* ſpeak-
ing of the Smuttineſs of ſome
Plays, *Bellinda* ſays,
*Why don't ſome Reformer or other
beat the Poet for it ?*
L. B. *Becauſe he is not ſo ſure of
our Private Approbation, as of our
Publick Thanks : Well, ſure there is
not upon Earth ſo impertinent a Thing
as Womens Modeſty.*
B. *Yes, Mens Fantaſque, that obli-
ges us to it : If we quit our Modeſty, they ſay we loſe our Charms ;
and yet they know That very Modeſty
is Affectation, and rail at our Hypo-
criſy.*

Now

Now which way this Gentleman will extract any thing from
hence, to the Difcouragement of
Modefty, is beyond my Chymi-
ftry: 'Tis plainly and directly the
contrary. Here are two Women
(not over Virtuous, as their whole
Character fhews), who being
alone, and upon the rallying Pin,
let fall a Word between Jeft and
Earneft, as if now and then they
found themfelves cramp'd by their
Modefty. But left this fhou'd
poffibly be miftaken by fome part
of the Audience, lefs apprehen-
five of Right and Wrong than the
reft, they are put in mind at the
fame Inftant, That (with the
Men) if they quit their Modefty,
they lofe their Charms: Now I
thought 'twas impoffible to put
the Ladies in mind of any thing
more likely to make 'em pre-
ferve it. I have nothing more
laid

laid to my Charge in the First
Chapter.

The Second is entituled, *The
Prophaneneſs of the Stage ;* which
he ranges under Two Heads.

Their Curſing and Swearing. And
*Their Abuſe of Religion and the
Holy Scriptures.*

As to *Swearing*, I agree with
him in what he ſays of it in general, That 'tis contrary both to Religion and Good Manners, eſpe-
cially before Women : But I ſay,
what he calls *Swearing* in the Play-
houſe, (at leaſt where I have to
anſwer for it) is a Breach upon
neither.

And here I muſt deſire the Reader to obſerve, His Accuſations
againſt me run almoſt always in
general Terms , he ſcarce ever
comes

comes to Particulars : I hope 'twill
be allow'd a good sign on my
side, that it always falls to my
turn to quote the thing at length
in my Defence, which he huddles
together in my Charge. What
follows will be an Instance of it.

He says in the 57th Page,
(where the Business of Swearing
is upon the *Tapis*) with a great
deal of Honesty and Charity,
That in this respect the *Relapse*
and the *Provok'd Wife* are particu-
larly rampant and scandalous.

Wou'd not any body imagine
from hence, that the Oaths that
were used there, were no less than
those of a Losing Bully at *Bag-
gammon*, or a Bilk'd Hackney-
Coachman ? Yet after all, the
stretch of the Prophaneness lies in
Lord *Foppington's Gad*, and Miss
Hoyden's I-Cod. This is all this
Gentleman's Zeal is in such a Fer-
ment about.   Now

Now whether such Words are entirely justifiable or not, there's this at least to be said for 'em; That People of the Nicest Rank both in their Religion and their Manners throughout *Christendom* use 'em.

In *France* you meet with *Par Die*, *Par Bleu*, *Ma Foy*, *&c.* in the constant Conversation of the Ladies and the Clergy, I mean those who are Religious even up to Bigotry it self; and accordingly we see they are always allow'd in their Plays: And in *England*, we meet with an Infinity of People, Clergy as well as Laity, and of the best Lives and Conversations, who use the Words *I-gad*, *I-faith*, *Codsfish*, *Cot's my Life*, and many more, which all lye liable to the same Objection.

Now whether they are right or wrong in doing it, I think at least
their

their Example is Authority enough
for the Stage ; and fhou'd have
been enough to have kept fo good
a Chriftian as Mr. *Collier* from
loading his Neighbour with fo
foul a Charge as Blafphemy and
Prophanenefs , unlefs he had
been better provided to make it
good.

The next thing he takes to task
in this Chapter, is the Abufe of
Religion and Holy Scripture.
Now here I think he fhou'd firft
clearly have prov'd, That no Story,
Phrafe , or Expreffion whatfoever
in the Scripture , whether in the
Divine, Moral, or Hiftorical part
of it, fhou'd be either repeated,
or fo much as alluded to , upon
the Stage, to how ufeful an End
foever it might be applied: This
I fay he fhou'd have firft put paft
a difpute, before he fell upon me
for an Abufer of the Holy Scri-
B   pture ;

pture; for unlefs that be to abufe
it, I am innocent.

The Scripture is made up of
Hiftory, Prophecy, and Precept;
which are things in their Nature
capable of no other Burlefque
than what calls in queftion either
their Reality or their Senfe: Now
if any Allufion I have made, be
found even to glance at either of
them, I fhall be ready to ask Pardon both of God and the Church.
But to the Trial.

The firft Accufation lies upon
P. 77. the *Provok'd Wife*, where *Rafor* is
highly blam'd by Mr. *Collier*; for,
in the 77th Page, pleading the
fame Excufe to an untoward
Prank he had newly play'd, which
Adam did heretofore upon a more
unfortunate Occafion: *That Wo-*
man having tempted him, the Devil
overcame him. How the Scripture
is affronted by this, I can't tell;
here's

here's nothing that reflects upon the Truth of the Story: It may indeed put the Audience in mind of their Forefather's Crime, and his Folly, which in my Opinion, like *Gunpowder-Treason*, ought never to be forgot.

The Line in *Rasor's* Confeſſion, Pro. W. which Mr. *Collier's* Modeſty ties P. 78. him from repeating, makes the Cloſe of this Sentence : *And if my Prayers were to be heard, her puniſh-ment for ſo doing ſhou'd be like the Serpent's of old, ſhe ſhou'd lye upon her face all the days of her life.*

All I ſhall ſay to this, is, That an Obſcene Thought muſt be buried deep indeed, if he don't ſmell it out ; and that I find he has a much greater Veneration for the Serpent than I have, who ſhall always make a very great diſtinction between my Reſpects to God and the Devil.

B 2   He

He runs a Muck at all. The
P. 78. next he launces at is my Lord *Foppington.* And here he's as angry at
me for being *for* Religion, as before for being *againſt* it, (which
ſhews you the Man's reſolv'd to
quarrel with me) : For I think his
Lordſhip's Words which he quotes
about St. *James's* Church, are beyond all diſpute on the Miniſter's
ſide, though not on his Congre-
gation's : The Indecencies of the
Place, the Levity of the Women,
and the unſeaſonable Gallantry of
Relapſe, the Men, are expos'd in the very
P. 23, 33. Lines this Gentleman is pleas'd to
quote for their Prophaneneſs. For
though my Lord *Foppington* is not
ſuppos'd to ſpeak what he does to
a Religious End, yet 'tis ſo or-
dered, that his manner of ſpeak-
ing it , together with the Character he repreſents , plainly and
obviouſly inſtructs the Audience
(even

(even to the meanest Capacity) that what he says of his Church-Behaviour, is design'd for their Contempt, and not for their Imitation: This is so notorious, that no School-boy cou'd mistake it: I therefore hope those who observe this Man of Reformation is capable of giving so good an Intention so pernicious a Turn, will conclude, when he sat down to write upon the Prophaneness of the Poets, he had nothing less in his Head, than to refine the Morals of the Age.

From the Elder Brother he falls upon the Younger; I suppose, because he takes me to be his Friend, for I find no other reason for his Quarrel: He accuses him for assuring his Man *Lory*, that he has kick'd his Conscience down Stairs; and he observes, he says, by the way, that this Loose Young Gen-

tleman

tleman is the Author's Favourite.
Now the Author obſerves by the
way, That he's always obſerving
wrong ; for he has no other proof
of his being his Favourite, than
that he has help'd him to a Wife,
who's likely to make his Heart
ake : But I ſuppoſe Mr. *Collier* is
of Opinion, that Gold can never
be bought too dear.

Relapſe,
p. 51.

The next Flirt is at *Worthy* and
Berinthia ; and here he tells you
Two Characters of Figure deter-
mine the Point in Defence of
Pimping. I can pardon his Miſtake in the buſineſs of Pimping,
becauſe I charitably believe the
Univerſity may have been the only
Place he has had any Experience
of it in, and there 'tis not mana-
ged indeed by People of any extraordinary Figure : But he may
be inform'd if he pleaſes, that in
this Righteous Town the Profeſ-
ſion

sion soars somewhat higher, and that (out of my Lord-Mayor's Liberties) there are such things as *Worthy* and *Berinthia* to be found. I brought 'em upon the Stage to shew the World how much the Trade was improv'd; but this Gentleman I find won't take my Word for't.

Nurse is to have the next Kick o' the Breech, and 'tis for being too Prophane. But that's left for me to quote again : For his part, all he repeats from her is, *That* Relapse, *his Worship (young Fashion) over-* P. 96. *flows with his Mercy and his Bounty : He is not only pleas'd to forgive us our Sins, but which is more than all, has prevail'd with me to become the Wife of thy Bosom.*

This he says is dull : Why so 'tis; and so is he, for thinking it worth his finding fault with, unless it had been spoke by some-

B 4   body

body elfe than a Nurfe, and to fome-
body elfe than Mr. *Bull*. But the
Prophane Stuff he fays precedes
it, I'll acquaint the Reader with.
She fays (fpeaking to the Chaplain) Roger, *Are not you a wicked
man*, Roger, *to fet your ftrength
againft a weak Woman, and perfuade
her it was no Sin to conceal Mifs's
Nuptials ? My Confcience flies in my
face for it, thou Prieft of* Baal ; *and
I find by woful Experience , thy Ab-
folution is not worth an old Caffock.*

The Reader may here be pleas'd
to take notice what this Gentleman would confter Prophanenefs, if he were once in the Sad-
dle with a good Pair of Spurs upon his Heels. I have all manner
of Refpect for the Clergy , but I
fhou'd be very forry to fee the Day,
that a Nurfe's cracking a Jeft upon a Chaplain (where it has no
Allufion to Religion) fhou'd be
brought

brought within the Verge of Prophaneneſs : But the next Chapter,
about the Abuſe of the Clergy,
will give occaſion for ſome more
Remarks of this kind.

Amanda comes next, I thought
ſhe might have ſcap'd, but it
ſeems with all her Vertue, ſhe
charges the Bible with Untruths,
and ſays,

Good Gods, what ſlippery ſtuff are
men compos'd of! ſure the Account
of their Creation's falſe, and 'twas
the Woman's Rib that they were
form'd of.

I'm ſorry the Gentleman who
writ this Speech of *Amanda's*, is not
here to defend himſelf; but he being gone away with the *Czar*, who
has made him Poet Laureat of
Muſcovy, I can do no leſs for the
Favour he intended me, than to
ſay this in his Juſtification. That
to my knowledge he has too much
Vene-

Veneration for the Bible, to in-
tend this a charge upon the Truth
of it; and that it appears very
plain to me, *Amanda* intended no
more to call it in queſtion by thoſe
words, than Mr. *Collier's* Wife
might be ſuppos'd to do, if from
ſome Obſervations upon his Book,
ſhe ſhou'd ſay, *Sure 'tis a miſtake
in the New Teſtament, that the fruits
of the Spirit are, Modeſty, Tempe-
rance, Juſtice, Meekneſs, Charity,*
&c. *for my* Jeremy *is a ſpiritual
Perſon, yet has not One of theſe
marks about him.*

P. 80.　　*Worthy* follows : And I am
threatned with no leſs than Eter-
nal Damnation, for making him
ſay to his Procureſs (when ſhe had
promis'd to do what he'd have
her) *Thou Angel of Light, let me
fall down and adore thee.* But I am
not commended for the Anſwer
ſhe makes him, to put the Audience

ence in mind, she was not suppos'd to deserve that Compli-
ment, *Thou Minister of Darkness* Relapse,
get up again, *for I hate to see the* P. 91.
Devil at his Devotions. If Mr. *Collier* had quoted this too, he had
given a better Character of me,
and I think of himself.

A Page or two farther, he has
a snap, as he goes by, at the *Provok'd Wife.* And here he's at foul Prov.
play again. He accuses Lady Wife,
Brute for setting down as a Pre- p. 3.
cept, that the Part of a Wife, is
to Cuckold her Husband; where-
as her words are these, *In short,
Bellinda, he has us'd me so barba-
rously of late, I cou'd almost resolve
to play the downright Wife, and
Cuckold him.*

This indeed is saying, Wives
do Cuckold their Husbands (I
ask the Ladies Pardons for Lying):
But 'tis not saying they shou'd do
so :

fo : I hope Mr. *Collier* will ask mine.

Lady *Brute* in her next Reply to *Bellinda*, fays, what I own at firft view feems much more liable to exception. Yet leaft the Audience fhou'd miftake her Raillery for her ferious Opinion, there is care taken immediately to inform 'em otherwife by making her reprimand her felf in thefe words to *Bellinda*. *But I fhall play the fool and jeft on, till I make you begin to think I am in earneft.*

Here, methinks, he fhou'd have commended me for my Caution. But he was furly, and wou'd not.

Young Fafhion is next accus'd for faying to *Lory* (when he had a profpect of getting Mifs *Hoyden*) *Providence, thou feeft at laft, takes care of men of Merit.*

This

This furely is a very poor Charge, and a Critick muſt be reduc'd to ſhort Commons to chop at it. Every body knows the word Providence in Common Diſcourſe goes for Fortune. If it be anſwer'd, Let it go for what it will, it is in ſtrictneſs God Almighty; I anſwer again, That if you go to ſtrictneſs, Fortune is God Almighty as much as Providence, and yet no One ever thought it Blaſphemy to ſay, Fortune's blind, or Fortune favours Fools: And the reaſon why it is not thought ſo, is becauſe 'tis known it is not meant ſo.

Berinthia comes again, and is blam'd for telling *Amanda*, *Worthy* had taken her to pieces like a Text, and preach'd upon every part of her; This is call'd a Lewd and Prophane Allegory. I confeſs it has at a glance, the appearance

ance of somewhat which it is not, and that methinks Mr. *Collier* might have been content to have charg'd it with; but he always takes care to stretch that way that becomes him least, and so is sure to be in the wrong himself, whether I am so or not.

Neither the Woman in general, nor any particular part about her, is liken'd to the Text; The Simile lies between the Manner of a Minister's using his Text, and *Worthy's* Flourishing upon his Mistress; So that the Prophanation's got in the wrong place here again. But supposing the Minister to be as Mr. *Collier* wou'd have him, as sacred a thing as his Text, there's nothing here that Burlesques him; 'Tis a Simile indeed, but a very inoffensive one, for it abuses nobody, and as to the Lewdness on't, I refer my self to the Reader
here

here again, whether this Gentleman does not give us another Instance of his having a very quick Nose, when some certain things are in the Wind. I believe, had the Obscenity he has routed up here, been buried as deep in his Church-yard, the Yarest Boar in his Parish wou'd hardly have tost up his Snout at it.

Berinthia's Close of her Speech, *Now consider of what has been said, and Heaven give you grace to put it in practice*, brings up the Rear of the Attack in this Chapter. These I own are words often us'd at the close of a Sermon, and therefore perhaps might as well have been let alone here. A known Pulpit-Expression sounds loose upon the Stage, though nothing is really affronted by it; for that I think in this Case is very plain, to any body that considers, who it is that

speaks

ſpeaks theſe words, and her manner of doing it. There's nothing
ſerious in't, as if ſhe wou'd per-
ſwade either *Amanda* or the Audience that Heaven approv'd what
ſhe was doing : 'Tis only a looſe
Expreſſion, ſuitable to the Character ſhe repreſents, which, throughout the Play, ſufficiently ſhews,
ſhe's brought upon the Stage to
Ridicule ſomething that's off
on't.

These three or four laſt Quotations Mr. *Collier* ſays are downright Blaſphemy, and within the
Law. I hope the Reader will
perceive he ſays wrong.

The next Chapter is upon the
Abuſe of the Clergy : And here
we are come to the Spring of the
Quarrel. I believe whoever reads
Mr. *Collier*, need take very little
pains to find out, that in all pro-
bability, had the Poets never diſ-
cover'd

cover'd a Rent in the Gown, he had done by Religion, as I do by my Brethren, left it to shift for it self.

In starting this Point, he opens a large Field for an Adversary to Rove in, he unbars the Gate of the Town, forgetting the Weakness of the Garrison; were I the Governor on't, I'd commend him for his Courage, much more than for his Prudence.

I once thought to have said a great deal upon this Occasion; But I have chang'd my mind, and will trouble the Reader with no more than I think is necessary to clear my self from the Charge of Ridiculing the Function of a Clergyman.

I am as fully convinc'd, as the most Pious Divine, or the most Refin'd Politician can wish me, how necessary the Practice of all

C   Moral

Moral Vertues is to our Happinefs
in this World, as well as to that
of another. And this Opinion has
its natural Confequence with me,
which is, to give me a regard to
every Inftrument of their Promo-
tion.

The Inftitution of the Clergy,
I own to be both in the Intention
and Capacity the moft effectual of
all; I have therefore for the Function all imaginable Deference,
and wou'd do all things to fup-
port it in fuch a kind of Credit, as
will render it moft formidable in
the execution of its Defign. But
in this Mr. *Collier* and I, I doubt,
are not like to agree.

He is of Opinion, That Riches
and Plenty, Title, State and Dominion, give a Majefty to Precept, and cry *Place* for it where-
ever it comes; That Chrift and
his Apoftles took the thing by the
wrong

wrong Handle ; and that the Pope and his Cardinals have much refin'd upon 'em in the Policy of Instruction. That shou'd a Vicar, like St. *John*, feed on Locusts and Wild Honey, his Parish wou'd think he had too ill a taste for himself, to cater for them ; and that a Bishop, who, like St. *Paul*, shou'd decline Temporal Dominion, wou'd shew himself such an Ass, his Advice wou'd go for nothing.

This I find is Mr. *Collier's* Opinion ; and if ever I take Orders, I won't swear it shan't be mine : But then I fear I shall continue in my Heresy ; Three Articles of which are these :

1. That the Shepherd, who has least Business at home in his House, is likely to take the most care of his Flock.

2. That

2. That he who finds fault with the Sauce he greedily fops his bread in, gives very good caufe to fufpect he'd fain keep it all to himfelf.

3. That he who is ftrict in the Performance of his Duty, needs no Other help, to be refpected in his Office.

These Pills, I own, are as bitter to the Flefh, as they are agreeable to the Spirit; but the Physick's found, and the Prefcription is fo neceffary, that when nothing elfe will perfuade fome people to fwallow 'em, I think 'tis not amifs, they fhou'd be forc'd down by the Stage. If any Poet has gone farther, let him anfwer for't; I'll endeavour to fhow I have not. And firft I'm to anfwer for Sir *John Brute*'s putting on a Gown to Abufe the Clergy.

If

If a Sir *John Brute* off the Stage
shou'd put on a Gown in his Cups,
and paſs his Lewdneſs upon the
World, for the Extravegances of a
Churchman; This, I own, wou'd
be an Abuſe and a Prejudice to
the Clergy. But to expoſe this
very Man upon the Stage, for
putting this Affront upon the
Gown; to put the Audience in
mind, that there were Laymen ſo
wicked, they car'd not what they
did to bring Religion in Contempt, and were therefore always
ready to throw dirt upon the Pi-
lots of it:

This I believe no body but a
Man of Mr. *Collier*'s heat, could have
miſtaken ſo much, to quote it under the head, of the Clergy abus'd
by the Stage. But Men that ride
Poſt, with the Reins looſe upon
the Neck, muſt expect to get falls.
When he writes again, he'll take

up

up perhaps, and mix a little Lead with his Quickſilver.

The Juſtice does indeed drop a word which alludes to the Jolly Doings of ſome Boon Companions in the Fenns; and if I had let him drop a word or two more, I think I had made him a better Juſtice than I have.

In the *Relapſe*, Mr. *Collier* complains that his Brother *Bull* wiſhes the married Couple Joy in Language ſo horribly ſmutty and Prophane, to tranſcribe it wou'd blot the Paper too much. I'm therefore put upon the old neceſſity to tranſcribe it for him, that the World may ſee what this honeſt Gentleman wou'd paſs upon them as well as me, for Prophane, had he as long a Sword in his Hand as the Pope has in his.

Bull's

Bull's words are thefe. *I moſt* Relapſe, *humbly thank your Honours*; *and I* P. 74. *hope, ſince it has been my Lot to join you in the Holy Bands of* Wedlock, *you will ſo cultivate the Soil, which I have crav'd a Bleſſing on, that your Children may ſwarm about you, like Bees about a Honey-comb.* Theſe are the words he calls horribly Smutty and Prophane.

The next Quarrel's about I don't know what; nor can light of any body that can tell me. He ſays, *Young Faſhion's* deſiring Mr. *Bull* to make haſte to Sir *Tunbelly*; He anſwers him very decently, *I fly* Relapſe, *my good Lord.* What this Gentle- P. 75. man means by this Quotation, I can't imagine; but I can anſwer for t'other Gentleman, he only meant he'd make haſte.

He quotes Two or Three Sen-tences more of *Bull's*, which are juſt as Prophane as the reſt: He

C 4 con-

concludes, That the Chaplain has a great deal of heavy Stuff upon his hands; and his chief Quarrel to me here is, That I have not made him a Wit.

I ask pardon, that I cou'd suppose a Deputy-Lieutenant's Chaplain cou'd be a Blockhead; but I thought, if there was such a thing, he was as likely to be met with in Sir *Tunbelly*'s House, as any where. If ever I write the Character of a Gentleman where a Chaplain like Mr. *Collier* is to have the Direction of the Family, I'll endeavour to give him more Sense, that I may qualify him for more Mischief.

He has now left lashing me in particular, and I only have my share in his general Stroke upon all such sinful Wretches, who *attack Religion under every Form, and pursue the Priesthood through all the Sub-*

Subdivisions of Opinion. He says, *Neither* Jews *nor* Heathens, Turks *nor* Christians, Rome *nor* Geneva, *Church nor Conventicle, can escape us.* And we say, They'll all escape us, if he can defend 'em. Priest or Presbyter, Pope or *Calvin*, *Mufti* or *Brammen*, Ambassador from God, or Envoy from the Devil, if they have but their Credentials from t'other World, they are (with him) all Brothers of the Sacred String; there's no more Discord than is necessary to make up the Harmony; and if a Poet does but touch the worst Instrument they play upon, the Holy Consort of Religion and Morality, he'll tell you, is quite out of Tune.

Thus violently does his Zeal to the Priesthood run away with him: Some Clergyman, methinks, should help to stop him; and I

almost

almoſt perſuade my ſelf there will : There is ſtill in the Gown of the Church of *England* a very great Number of Men , both Learned, Wiſe, and Good , who thoroughly underſtand Religion, and truly love it : From amongſt theſe I flatter my ſelf ſome Hero will ſtart up, and with the naked Virtue of an Old Generous *Roman*, appear a Patriot for Religion indeed ; with a Trumpet before him proclaim the Secrets of the Cloyſter, and by diſcovering the Diſeaſe, guide the World to the Cure on't.

He may ſhew (if he pleaſes), That the Contempt of the Clergy proceeds from another kind of Want, than that of Power and Revenue : That Piety and Learning, Charity and Humility, with ſo viſible a Neglect of the Things of this Life , that no one can
doubt

doubt their Expectations from another; is the way to be believ'd in their Doctrine, follow'd in their Precepts, and (by a moſt infallible Conſequence) reſpected in their Function. Religion is not a Cheat, and therefore has no need of Trappings : Its Beauty is in its Nature, and wants no Dreſs : An Ambaſſador who comes with Advantagious Propoſals, ſtands in no need of Equipage to procure him Reſpect. He who teaches Piety and Morality to the World, is ſo great a Benefactor to Mankind, he need never doubt their Thanks, if he does not ask too much of their Money. But here's the Sand, where Religion runs aground, Avarice and Ambition in its Teachers, áre the Rocks on which 'tis daſh'd to pieces. It, with many weak people, brings the whole matter into doubt. Men

natu-

naturally suspect the Foundation
of a Project, where the Projector
is eager for a larger Contribution
than they see is necessary to carry
on the Work. But this Case is so
plain, there needs nothing to il-
lustrate it. 'Tis the Clergy's In-
vasion into the Temporal Dominion, that has rais'd the Alarm
against 'em : It has made their
Doctrine suspected, and by consequence, their Persons despis'd.
I own I have sometimes doubted
whether *Pharaoh* with all the Hard-
ness of his Heart, wou'd have pur-
su'd the Children of *Israel* to the
Red Sea, as he did, if they had
not meddled with the Riches of
his Subjects at their parting ; but
that Action renew'd the Doubts of
a Faith so weak as his, and made
him, in spight of all the Miracles
he had seen, question whether
Moses had his Commission from
God.

God. He paid indeed for his Infidelity, as others may happen to do upon a parallel Mistake, I wish none have don't already: But I'm afraid those very Instances Mr. *Collier* gives us of the Grandeur of the Clergy, are the things that have destroy'd both them and their Flocks.

They owe their Fall to their Ambition; their soaring so high has melted their Wings; in a word, had they never been so great, they had never been so little. But lest I shou'd be mistaken, and make my self Enemies of Men I am no Enemy to, I must declare, my Thoughts are got to *Rome*, while I am talking thus of the Clergy; for the Charge is in no measure so heavy at home. The Reformation has reduc'd things to a tolerable Medium; and I believe what Quarrel we

have

have to our Clergy here, points
more at the Conduct of some,
than the Establishment of the
whole. I wish it may never go
farther, and I believe it won't, if
those who I don't question are still
by much the Majority, will to so
good an End (as the curbing
their Ambitious Brethren, and reforming their Lewd ones) for
once make a League with the
Wicked, and agree, That whilst
They play their Great Artillery at
'em from the Pulpit, the Poets
shall pelt 'em with their Small Shot
from the Stage. But since Mr. *Collier* is violently bent against this,
I'll tell him why I am for it. And
'tis,

Because he has put me in mind,
in the first Words of his Book,
That the Business of Plays, *is to
recommend Virtue and discountenance
Vice: To shew the Uncertainty of
Human*

Human Greatness ; the sudden Turns of Fate, and the unhappy Conclusions of Violence and Injustice : That 'tis to expose the Singularities of Pride and Fancy; to make Folly and Falshood contemptible, and to bring every thing that is ill, under Infamy and Neglect.

The next Chapter is upon the Encouragement of Immorality by the Stage : And here *Constant* is fallen upon, for pretending to be a Fine Gentleman, without living up to the Exact Rules of Religion. If Mr. *Collier* excludes every one from that Character, that does not, I doubt he'll have a more general Quarrel to make up with the Gentlemen of *England*, than I have with the Lords, tho' he tells 'em I have highly affronted 'em.

But I wou'd fain know after all, upon what Foundation he lays so positive

positive a Position, That *Constant* is my Model for a Fine Gentleman ; and that he is brought upon the Stage for Imitation.

He might as well say, if I brought His Character upon the Stage, I design'd it a Model to the Clergy : And yet I believe most People wou'd take it t'other way. O, but these kind of Fine Gentlemen , he says , are always prosperous in their Undertakings, and their Vice under no kind of Detection ; for in the Fifth Act of the Play, they are usually rewarded with a Wife or a Mistress. And suppose I shou'd reward him with a Bishoprick in the Fifth Act, wou'd that mend his Character ? I have too great a Veneration for the Clergy, to believe that wou'd make 'em follow his steps. And yet (with all due Respect to the Ladies) take one Amour with
another,

another, the Bishoprick may prove as weighty a Reward as a Wife or a Mistress either. He says, Mr. *Bull* was abus'd upon the Stage, yet he got a Wife and a Benefice too. Poor *Constant* has neither, nay, he has not got even his Mistress yet, he had not, at least, when the Play was last Acted. But this honest Doctor, I find, does not yet understand the Nature of Comedy, tho' he has made it his Study so long. For the Business of Comedy is to shew People what they shou'd do, by representing them upon the Stage, doing what they shou'd not. Nor is there any necessity a Philosopher shou'd stand by, like an Interpreter at a Poppet-show, to explain the Moral to the Audience: The Mystery is seldom so deep, but the Pit and Boxes can dive into it; and 'tis their Example out of the

D   Play-

Play-house, that chiefly influences
the Galleries. The Stage is a
Glass for the World to view it self
in ; People ought therefore to see
themselves as they are ; if it makes
their Faces too Fair, they won't
know they are Dirty, and by consequence will neglect to wash 'em :
If therefore I have shew'd *Constant*
upon the Stage, what generally
the Thing call'd a Fine Gentleman
is off on't, I think I have done
what I shou'd do. I have laid
open his Vices as well as his Vir-
tues : 'Tis the Business of the Audience to observe where his Flaws
lessen his Value; and by consi-
dering the Deformity of his Ble-
mishes, become sensible how
much a Finer Thing he wou'd be
without 'em. But after all, *Constant* says nothing to justify the
Life he leads, except where he's
pleading with Lady *Brute* to debauch

bauch her; and fure no body will
fuppofe him there to be fpeaking
much of his Mind. Befides, his
Miftrefs in all her Anfwers makes
the Audience obferve the Fallacy
of his Arguments. And I think
Young Ladies may without much
Penetration make this ufe of the
Dialogue, That they are not to
take all for Gofpel, Men tell 'em
upon fuch occafions.

The *Provok'd Wife* is charg'd
with nothing more, except *Bellinda*
for declaring fhe'd be glad of
a Gallant, and Lady *Brute* for
faying, *Virtue's an Afs, and a Gallant's worth forty on't.*

I need make no other Defence
for the Ladies, than I have already done for the Gentlemen, the
Cafe being much the fame. However, to fhew how unfair an Ad-
verfary I have to deal with, I muft
acquaint the Reader, That *Bellin-*

da

da only *says*, *If her Pride shou'd make her marry a Man she hated, her Virtue wou'd be in danger from the Man she lov'd.* Now her Reflection upon this, I take to be a useful Caution both to Mothers and Daughters (who think Chastity a Virtue) to consider something in their Matches, besides a Page and a Coronet.

Lady *Brute*'s Words are fairly recited, but wrongly apply'd : Mr. *Collier*'s mistaken ; 'tis not Virtue she exposes, but her self, when she says 'em : Nor is it me he exposes, but himself, when he quotes 'em.

He gives me no farther occasion to mention the *Provok'd Wife*, I'll therefore take this to make an Observation or two upon the Moral of it, it being upon that account he has call'd it in question, and

and endeavour'd to make it pafs
for a Play that has none.

This Play was writ many years
ago, and when I was very young;
if therefore there had been fome
fmall Flaws in the Moral, I might
have been excus'd for the Writing,
tho' liable to fome Blame for the
Publifhing it. But I hope it is
not fo loofe, but I may be pardon'd for Both, whether Mr. *Collier* fets his Seal to't or not.

As for Sir *John Brute*, I think
there are an Infinity of Husbands
who have a very great fhare of
his Vices : And I think his Bufi-
nefs throughout the Play, is a vi-
fible Burlefque upon his Chara-
&ter. 'Tis this Gentleman that
gives the Spring to the reft of the
Adventures: And tho'I own there
is no mighty Plot in the whole
matter, yet what there is, tends
to the Reformation of Manners.

D 3   For

For besides the hateful Idea his
Figure needs must give of his
Character, the ill Consequence
of his Brutality appears in the
Miscarriage of his Wife : For tho'
his ill usage of her does not justify
her Intrigue, her intriguing upon
his ill usage, may be a Caution
for some. I don't find our Women in *England* have much of the
Muscovite Temper in 'em: If you'll
make 'em think you are their
Friend, you must give 'em softer
strokes of your Kindness; if you
don't, the Gallant has a dange-
rous Plea, and such a one as, I
doubt, has carri'd many a Cause.
Religion, I own, (when a Woman has it) is a very great Bul-
wark for her Husband's Security :
And so is Modesty, and so is Fear,
and so is Pride; and yet all are
little enough, if the Gallant has
a Friend in the Garison. I therefore

fore think That Play has a very good End , which puts the Governor in mind, let his Soldiers be ever so good , 'tis possible he may provoke 'em to a Mutiny.

The rest of the Characters, as they have no very great good, so they have very little mischief in 'em. Lady *Fanciful* is ridicul'd for her Vanity and her Affectation. *Mademoiselle* brings to mind what may often be expected from a *Suivante* of her Countrey. *Heartfree* is catch'd for his extravagant Railing at Womankind : And *Constant* gives himself a great deal of trouble, for a thing that is not worth his Pains. In short, they are most of 'em busy about what they shou'd not be; and those who observe they are so, may take warning to employ their time better.

I have

I have nothing more to anſwer for in this Chapter, but making the Women ſpeak againſt their own Sex: And having the Preſumption to bring a Fop upon the Stage with the Title of a Lord.

This is a bungling Piece of Policy, to make the Women and the Nobility take up Arms in his Quarrel. I'm aſham'd a Churchman ſhou'd ſpin his Miſchief no finer: The Sollicitors to the Holy War had almoſt as good a Plea. But he had one Conſideration farther in this: He remember'd he had poſitively declar'd, Let a Clergyman be guilty of what Crimes he wou'd, he was God's Ambaſſador, and therefore a Privileg'd Perſon, whom the Poets ought never to take into Cuſtody. This, upon ſecond thoughts, he found wou'd hardly go down, if he monopoliz'd the Privilege to them alone; and

and so left the Company shou'd
bring their Charter to a Dispute,
he has open'd the Books for New
Subscriptions ; the Lords and the
Ladies are invited to come in ; the
Gentlemen, I suppose, may do so
too, if they please ; and, in short,
rather than the Committee of Religion shall be expos'd for their
Faults, all Mankind shall be admitted to Trade in Sin as they
please.

But I dare answer for the Laity,
of what Quality soever they may
be, they are willing their Vices
shou'd be scourg'd upon the
Stage ; at least, I never yet heard
one of 'em declare the contrary.
If the Clergy insist upon being
exempted by themselves, I believe
they may obtain it : But I'm apt
to fancy, if they protect their
Loose Livers from being expos'd
in the Play-house, they'll find 'em

grow

grow the bolder to expose themselves in the Streets. A Clergyman is not in any Countrey exempted from the Gallows : And
Mr. *Collier* has seen one of his
Brethren peep through a worse
Place than a Garret-Window :
Nay, (in a Reign he reckons a
Just One) amble through the
Town at the Tayl of a Cart,
with his Sins in Red Letters upon
his Shoulders. A Hangman then
may jerk him; Why not a Poet ?
Perhaps 'tis fear'd he might give
him more Sensible Strokes.

I am now come to thank the
Gentleman for the last of his Favours; in which he is so generous
to bestow a Chapter entire upon
me.

I'm extremely oblig'd to him
for it, since 'tis more than ever he
promis'd me; For in the Title of
his Book, he designs to Correct
the

the Stage only for the Immorality
and Prophaneneſs of it. And indeed I think that was all his buſineſs with't. But he has ſince con-
ſider'd better of the matter, and
rather than *quit his hold*, falls a
Criticizing upon Plots, Characters,
Words, Dialogue, &c. even to
telling us, when our fine Gentlemen make Love in the prevail-
ing Strein, and when not. This
gives us a farther view of his Stu-
dies; but, I think, if he kept to
his Text, he had given us a better View of a Clergyman.

It may, perhaps, be expected
I ſhou'd ſay more in anſwer to
this Chapter, than to all that has
gone before it; the Senſe of the
Play being attack'd here, much
more than the Moral, which thoſe
who will take Mr. *Collier*'s word
for my Principles, muſt believe I
am leaſt concern'd for. But I ſhall
ſatisfy

satisfy 'em of the contrary, by leaving the Sense to answer for it self if it can : I'll only say this for't in general ; That it looks as if a Play were not overloaded with Blunders, when so Pains-taking a Corrector is reduc'd to the wretched necessity of spending his Satyr upon *Fire* and *Flames*, being in the same Line ; and *Arms* twice in the same Speech, though at six lines distance one from t'other. This looks as if the Critick were rather duller than the Poet : But when men fight in a Passion, 'tis usual to make insignificant Thrusts ; most of his are so wide, they need no parrying ; and those that hit, are so weak, they make no Wound.

I don't pretend however to have observ'd the nicety of Rule in this Play ; I writ it in as much haste (though not in so much fu

ry)

ry) as he has done his Remarks upon't; 'Tis therefore poſſible I may have made as many fooliſh Miſtakes.

I cou'd however ſay a great deal againſt the too exact obſervance of what's call'd the Rules of the Stage, and the crowding a Comedy with a great deal of Intricate Plot. I believe I cou'd ſhew, that the chief entertainment, as well as the Moral, lies much more in the Characters and the Dialogue, than in the Buſineſs and the Event. And I can aſſure Mr. *Collier*, if I wou'd have weakned the Diverſion, I cou'd have avoided all his Objections, and have been at the expence of much leſs pains than I have : And this is all the Anſwer I ſhall make to 'em, except what tumbles in my way, as I'm obſerving the foul play he ſhews me, in ſetting
the

the *Relapse* in so wrong a Light as he does, at his opening of the Fable on't.

In the first Page of his Remarks upon this Play, he says I have given it a wrong Title ; The *Relapse*, or *Vertue in Danger*, relating only to *Loveless* and *Amanda*, who are Characters of an Inferior Consideration ; and that the *Younger Brother*, or the *Fortunate Cheat* had been much more proper ; because *Young Fashion* is, without competition, the principal Person in the Comedy.

In reading this Gentleman's Book, I have been often at loss to know when he's playing the Knave, and when he's playing the Fool ; nor can I decide which he's at now. But this I'm sure, *Young Fashion* is no more the Principal Person of the Play, than He's the best Character in

the

the Church; nor has he any reason to suppose him so, but because he brings up the Rear of the most insignificant part of the Play, and happens to be the Bridegroom in the close on't.

I won't say any thing here irreverently of Matrimony, because *à la Françoise* Bigottry runs high, and by all I see, we are in a fair way to make a Sacrament on't again. But this I may say, That I had full as much respect for *Young Fashion*, while he was a Batchellor, and yet I think while he was so, *Loveless* had a part, that from People who desire to be the better for Plays, might draw a little more Attention. In short; My Lord *Fopington*, and the *Bridegroom*, and the *Bride*, and the *Justice*, and the *Matchmaker*, and the *Nurse*, and the *Parson* at the rear of 'em, are the Inferior Persons of the Play (I
mean

mean as to their business) and what they do, is more to divert the Audience, by something particular and whimsical in their Humours, than to instruct 'em in any thing that may be drawn from their Morals; though several useful things may in passing be pickt up from 'em too.

This is as distinct from the main intention of the Play, as the business of *Gomez* is in the *Spanish Fryar*. I shan't here enter into the Contest, whether it be right to have two distinct Designs in one Play; I'll only say, I think when there are so, if they are both entertaining, then 'tis right; if they are not, 'tis wrong. But the Dispute here is, Where lies the principal business in the *Relapse*? Mr. *Collier* decides it roundly for the Wedding-house, because there's best Chear; his Patron, Sir *Tunbelly*, has got a good
Venison-

Venison-Pasty for him, and such
a Tankard of Ale, as has made
him quite forget the Moral Reflections he shou'd have made upon
the Disorders that are slipt into
Loveless's House, by his being too
positive in his own strength, and
forgetting, that *Lead us not into
Temptation*, is a Petition in our
Prayers, which was thought fit to
be tackt to that for our daily Bread.

And here my Design was such,
I little thought it wou'd ever have
been Ridicul'd by a Clergyman.
'Twas in few words this.

I observ'd in a Play, call'd *Love's
last Shift, or the Fool in Fashion*, a
Debauche pay so dear for his Lewdness, and his Folly, as from a plen-
tiful Fortune, and a Creditable E-
stablishment in the World, to be
reduc'd by his Extravagance to
want even the Common Supports
of Life.

E   In

In this Diſtreſs, Providence (I ask Mr. *Collier*'s pardon for uſing the word) by an unexpected turn in his favour, reſtores him to Peace and Plenty : And there is that in the manner of doing it, and the Inſtrument that brings it to paſs, as muſt neceſſarily give him the moſt ſenſible View, both of his Miſery paſt, from the Looſeneſs of his Life ; and his Happineſs to come, in the Reform of it. In the cloſe of the Play, he's left throughly convinc'd it muſt therefore be done, and as fully determin'd to do it.

For my part, I thought him ſo undiſputably in the right ; and he appear'd to me to be got into ſo agreeable a Tract of Life, that I often took a pleaſure to indulge a muſing Fancy, and ſuppoſe my ſelf in his place. The Happineſs I ſaw him poſſeſt of, I lookt upon as

a Jewel

a Jewel of a very great worth, which naturally lead me to the fear of losing it; I therefore considr'd by what Enemies 'twas most likely to be attack'd, and that directed me in the Plan of the Works that were most probable to defend it. I saw but one danger in Solitude and Retirement, and I saw a thousand in the bustle of the World; I therefore in a moment determin'd for the Countrey, and suppos'd *Lovelace* and *Amanda* gone out of Town.

I found these Reflections of some service to my self, and so (being drawn into the folly of writing a Play) I resolv'd the Town shou'd share 'em with me. But it seems they are so little to Mr. *Collier's* Taste, he'll neither eat the Meat himself, nor say Grace to't for any body else. I'll try however if

the

the following Account will recommend it to him.

Loveless and his Wife appear in the start of the Play, happy in their Retirement, and in all Human Prospect, likely to continue so, if they continue where they are. As for *Amanda*, she's so pleas'd with her Solitude, she desires never to leave it; and the Adventures that happen upon her being forc'd to it, may caution a Husband (if he pleases) against being so very importunate to bring his Wife (how vertuous soever) into the way of Mischief, when she her self is content to keep out of it.

Loveless, He's so thoroughly wean'd from the taste of his Debauches, he has not a thought toward the Stage where they us'd to be acted. 'Tis Business, not Pleasure, brings him thither again, and his Wife can't persuade him there's

there's the leaſt danger of a Relapſe ; He's proud to think on
what a Rock his Reformation is
built, and reſolves She her ſelf
ſhall be a Witneſs, That though
the Winds blow, and the Billows
roar, yet nothing can prevail a-
gainſt it.

To Town in ſhort they come,
and Temptation's ſet at defi-
ance. *Lead us not into it*, is a
Requeſt he has no farther occaſion for. The firſt place he tries
his Strength, is where he us'd to
be the moſt ſenſible of his Weak-
neſs.

He cou'd reſiſt no Woman
heretofore ; He'll now ſhew he
can ſtand a Battalion of 'em ; ſo
to the Play-houſe he goes, and
with a ſmile of contempt looks
cooly into the Boxes. But *Berinthia* is there to chaſtiſe his Preſumption : He diſcovers her Beau-

E 3   ty,

ty, but defpifes her Charms; and
is fond of himfelf, that fo un-
mov'd he can confider 'em. He
finds a Pleafure indeed, in view-
ing the Curiofity., but 'tis only
to contemplate the Skill of the
Contriver. As for Defire, he's
fatisfy'd he has none; let the
Symptoms be what they will, he's
free from the Difeafe; he may
gaze upon the Lady till he grows
a Statue in the Place, but he's
fure he's in love with none but his
Wife. Home he comes, and gives
her an account of what he had feen;
fhe's alarm'd at the Story, and
looks back to her Retirement : He
blames her Sufpicion, and all's
filent again. When Fate (here's
Blafphemy again) fo difpofes
things, that the Temptation's
brought home to his Door, and
his Wife has the misfortune to in-
vite it into her Houfe. In fhort;
Berinthia

Berinthia becomes one of the Family : She's Beautiful in her Perfon, Gay in her Temper, Coquet in her Behaviour, and Warm in her Defires. In a word, The Battery is fo near, there's no ftanding the Shot, Conftancy's beaten down; the Breach is made, Refolution gives ground, and the Town's taken.

This I defign'd for a natural Inftance of the Frailty of Mankind, even in his moft fixt Determinations; and for a mark upon the defect of the moft fteady Refolve, without that neceffary Guard, of keeping out of Temptation. But I had ftill a farther end in *Lovelefs's Relapfe*, and indeed much the fame with that in the *Provok'd Wife*, though in different kind of Characters; thefe latter being a little more refin'd,

E 4   which

which places the Moral in a more reasonable, and I think a more agreeable View. There; The Provocation is from a *Brute*, and by consequence cannot be suppos'd to sting a Woman so much, as if it had come from a more Reasonable Creature; the Lady therefore that gives her self a Loose upon it, cou'd not naturally be represented the best of her Sex. Virtuous (upon some ground or other) there was a Necessity of making her; but it appears by a Strain of Levity that runs through her Discourse, she ow'd it more to Form, or Apprehension, or at best to some few Notions of Gratitude to her Husband, for taking her with an Inferior Fortune, than to any Principle of Religion, or an extraordinary Modesty. 'Twas therefore not extremely to be wondred at, that when her Husband made

made her House uneasy to her at home, she shou'd be prevail'd with to accept of some Diversions abroad. However, since she was Regular while he was kind, the Fable may be a useful Admonition to Men who have Wives, and wou'd keep 'em to themselves, not to build their Security so entirely upon their Ladies Principles, as to venture to pull from under her all the Political Props of her Virtue.

But in the Adventures of *Loveless* and *Amanda*, the Caution is carri'd farther. Here's a Woman whose Virtue is rais'd upon the utmost Strength of Foundation: Religion, Modesty, and Love, defend it. It looks so Sacred, one wou'd think no Mortal durst approach it; and seems so fix'd, one wou'd believe no Engine cou'd shake it: Yet loosen one Stone, the

the Weather works in, and the Structure molders apace to decay. She difcovers her Husband's return to his Inconftancy. The unfteadinefs of his Love gives her a Contempt of his Perfon; and what leffens her Opinion, declines her Inclination. As her Paffion for him is abated, that againft him's inflam'd; and as her Anger increafes, her Reafon's confus'd : Her Judgment in diforder, her Religion's unhing'd; and that Fence being broken, fhe lies widely expos'd : *Worthy*'s too fenfible of the Advantage, to let flip the Occafion : He has Intelligence of the Vacancy, and puts in for the Place.

Poor *Amanda*'s perfuaded he's only to be her Friend, and that all he asks, is to be admitted as a Comforter in her Afflictions. But when People are fick, they are fo fond of a Cordial, that when they get it to
their

their Nose, they are apt to take too much on't.

She finds in his Company such a Relief to her Pain , she desires the Physician may be always in her sight. She grows pleas'd with his Person as well as his Advice, yet she's sure he can never put her Virtue in Danger. But she might have remembred her Husband was once of the same Opinion; and have taken warning from him, as the Audience, I intended, shou'd do from 'em both.

This was the Design of the Play; which I think is something of so much greater Importance than *Young Fashion*'s marrying Miss *Hoyden*, that if I had call'd it the *Younger Brother*, or the *Fortunate Cheat*, instead of *the Relapse*, or *Virtue in danger*, I had been just as much in the wrong, as Mr. *Collier* is now.

His

His reason, I remember, why *Loveless* can't be reckon'd a Principal Part, is, Because he sinks in the Fourth Act. But I can tell him, If the Play had sunk in the Fourth Act too, it had been better than 'tis, by just Twenty *per Cent.* However, tho' *Loveless*'s Affair is brought about in the Fourth Act, *Amanda*'s last Adventure is towards the End of the Fifth. But this is only a Cavil from the Formality of the Criticks; which is always well broken into, if the Diversion's increas'd by't, and Nature not turn'd Top-side-turvy. If therefore nothing but the Criticks (I mean such as Mr. *Collier*) find themselves shock'd by the Disorders of this Play, I think I need trouble my self as little to justify what's past, as I own I shou'd to mend it, in any thing to come; had I thoughts of medling any

more

more with the Stage. But to
draw to an End.

I have reserv'd for the Close of
this Paper, one Observation (a
home one I think) upon the Unfair Dealing of this Reverend
Gentleman; which shews at once
the Rancor of his Venom, the
Stretch of his Injustice, and by a
Moral Consequence, I think, the
Extremity of his Folly: For sure
there cannot be a greater, than for
a Man of his Coat, at the very
Instant he's declaiming against the
Crimes of the Age, to lay himself so open, to be hit in the most
Immoral Blot of Life, which that
of Slander undisputably is.

To Explain. I beg the Reader
will bestow one Moments Reflection upon the Pains he has taken to
make *Young Fashion* and his Affair
pass for the Principal Concern of
the Comedy; which he only has
done,

done, in hopes to sink the useful Moral of the Play, which he knew lay in t'other part of it, and wou'd unavoidably have appear'd in Judgment against his Reflections upon the whole, if he had not taken this way to stifle the Evidence: He therefore carries on the Imposture to that degree, as at last to slubber over the Conclusive Scene between *Worthy* and *Amanda*, as if there were no Meaning of Importance in it. Nay, his Rage is so great (to find the Stamp of Immorality he wou'd fain have fix'd upon this Play, so cleanly wash'd off by the Close of this Scene) that he cares not what Folly he commits: And therefore in his Heats, rather than commend it for the Alarm it gives to Lewdness, by *Worthy's* Reflections upon *Amanda's* Refusal, he turns him into Ridicule for an

Insipid

Inſipid *Platonick* : By which we may gueſs, had he been in the Fine Gentleman's Place, the Lady wou'd not have 'ſcap'd as ſhe did. I'll repeat *Worthy*'s Words, with the Doctor's uſe of 'em, and ſo have done.

Sure there's Divinity about her, and ſh'as diſpenc'd ſome Portion on't to me : For what but now was the Wild Flame of Love, or (to diſſect that ſpecious Term) the vile, the groſs Deſires of Fleſh and Blood , is in a Moment turn'd to Adoration : The courſer Appetite of Nature's gone, and 'tis methinks the Food of Angels I require. How long this Influence may laſt , Heaven knows : But in this Moment of my Purity, I cou'd on her Own Terms accept her Heart. Yes, Lovely Woman, I can accept it, for now 'tis doubly worth my Care : Your Charms are much increas'd ſince thus adorn'd: When Truth's ex- Relapſe, P. 100.

torted

torted from us, then we own the *Robe
of Virtue is a Graceful Habit.*

Cou'd Women but our *secret Councils
    scan ;*
Cou'd they but reach the deep *Reserves
    of Man ;*
They'd wear it on, that that of Love
    might last :
For when they throw off one, we soon
    the other cast.
Their Sympathy is such-----
The Fate of one, the other scarce can
    fly,
They live together, and together dye.

This Reflection *Worthy* makes
to himself, upon *Amanda's* having
Virtue enough to resist him, when
he plainly saw she lay under a
pressing Temptation.

Now when 'tis consider'd, That
upon the Stage the Person who
speaks in a Soliloquy is always
                        suppos'd

suppos'd to deliver his real Thoughts to the Audience : I think it muſt be granted, there never was a homer Check given to the Lewdneſs of Women in any Play whatſoever. For what in Nature can touch 'em nearer, than to ſee a man, after all the Pains he has taken, and the Eager Arguments he has us'd, lay open his Heart, and frankly confeſs, had he gain'd his Miſtreſs, ſhe had loſt her Gallant.

This I thought was a Turn ſo little ſuited to Comedy, that I confeſs I was afraid the Rigor of the Moral wou'd have damn'd the Play. But it ſeems every body cou'd reliſh it but a Clergyman. Mr. *Collier's* Words are theſe :

Amanda continues obſtinate, and P. 227.
is not in the uſual Humour of the Stage : Upon this, like a well-bred Lover he ſeizes her by force, and

F   *threat-*

threatens to kill her : (By the way,
this Purblind Divine might have
feen 'twas himfelf, not his Miftrefs,
he threatned.) *In this Rencounter
the Lady proves too nimble, and flips
through his Fingers. Upon this Dif-
appointment he cries* , There's Divinity about her , and fhe has
difpens'd fome Portion on't to me.
*His Paffion is metamorphos'd in the
turn of a band : He's refin'd into a*
Platonick *Admirer, and goes off as
like a Town-Spark as you wou'd wifh.
And fo much for the Poet's Fine Gentleman.*

The World may fee by this,
what a Contempt the Doctor has
for a Spark that can make no better ufe of his Miftrefs, than to ad-
mire her for her Virtue. This
methinks is fomething fo very extraordinary in a Clergyman, that
I almoft fancy when He and I are
faft afleep in our Graves, thofe who
fhall

ſhall read what we both have pro-
duc'd, will be apt to conclude
there's a Miſtake in the Tradition
about the Authors; and that'twas
the Reforming Divine writ the
Play, and the Scandalous Poet
the Remarks upon't.

F I N I S.